Purcell's Cove

The Little Place that Helped Build Halifax City

Elsie (Purcell) Millington

Canadian Cataloguing in Publication Data

Millington, Elsie, 1924-
    Purcell's Cove

    ISBN 1-895332-25-7

    1. Purcells Cove (Halifax, N.S.)--History. I. Title.
FC2349.P87M54 2000   971.6'225   C00-910562-X
F1039.5.P87M54 2000

Book Design by Desktop Publishing Ltd.   Victoria

Dedicated lovingly to Lawrence (Larry) Bellefontaine.
He loved the Cove.

Acknowledgements

I gratefully acknowledges the support of many, many people: family members, in particular sister Olive who cared for the family so efficiently and lovingly when mother died, providing me (seven at the time) with a wonderfully happy childhood; Vincent and Diane Purcell, the nephew and niece who live in a home on the land where I was born and who inspired me to write this book; Iris Shea, who had done some genealogical research on the family and who had recovered some early photos of the Purcell's Cove quarries; to Gertrude Story, the creative writing instructor who helped and encouraged me with this book; and to Jim Bisakowski of Desktop Publishing Ltd. who put it all together.

Grateful acknowledgments as well to : *Sketches and traditions of the Northwest Arm* by John W. Regan; Public Archives of Nova Scotia (PANS), with special appreciation to Gary Shotlak for his help; Mainland South Heritage Society; Spring Garden Road Memorial Library Reference Department; and the Maritime Museum of the Atlantic.

A special thank you to the following individuals: Rod MacLean, Judith Gorham, Doris MacLean, Muriel Purcell, Clare Parks, Ruth Iceton, Hilda Tanner, Wayne Purcell, Bridget Purcell, Annie Liggins Welch, George Hebb, Allan Ruffman, Lynn Simpson, Terry Shaw, Phyllis Fenerty, Edward Liggins and Jim Clark.

CONTENTS

1
Purcell's Cove: The Little Place that Helped Build Halifax City

North end of The Cove. (Hilda Lyons Tanner)

Growing up in Purcell's Cove, the favourite saying was, "When our Lord created the world, He had a lot of rocks left over and placed them in the Cove."

We never gave a thought to the history of the surrounding quarries. They were just a pile of rocks. Our thoughts would more likely be on how warm the water was so we could go swimming in the cove.

On the 24th day of May, Queen Victoria's birthday, it was customary to take a quick dip. We would always test the temperature. If frigid, we certainly did not stay in the water too long.

Also, on that day, rain or shine, we would go for a hike along the road near the rocky seaside, visiting lighthouses and other little coves along the way.

Purcell's Cove is situated at the mouth of the

Northwest Arm of the historic Halifax Harbour. At first it was called Mackerel Cove, probably by the First Nations people. A small inlet situated near the quarries was named Indian Cove, and there was also a trail they called Indian Path which they used to get to the lakes, beyond the boundaries of the quarries. It is said they used the cove area to fish and celebrate festivals.

In 1752, William Russell Esquire was granted a parcel of land that included the cove and island, which were renamed for this William Russell.

In 1828 Samuel Purcell purchased the Russell grant of 300 acres and island for 200 pounds. At that time the name was changed to Purcell's Cove.

This Samuel was the son of another Samuel Purcell, an ex-service man from England, who in 1770 had received a grant of land at Portuguese Cove, where his son, the buyer of the Russell grant, was born.

Purcell's Cove with dawn breaking over Halifax Harbour.

Purcell's Cove

In 1793 Samuel Purcell, Jr. had married a Portuguese Cove girl, Mary Verge, and they eventually moved their family to Purcell's Cove.

Mary, who went to her just reward in 1851, is still remembered as the Mother of the Cove.

The obituary in the paper of the times says of her, "She was deeply beloved and highly respected; when living, her home was the home of the stranger; her hospitality knew no bounds. She left an example to her children's children which will last as an ever-refreshing memento of her excellent worth. She died as she lived, in peace with all and in the hope of a blessed immortality."

The Cove with Halifax Harbour in the background.   (Hilda Lyons Tanner)

2
Purcell Family in the Cove:
Aunt Alice

At far right is the Purcell Family home which eventually became Iceton's Store.

When, in about the year 1828, Samuel Purcell Jr. and his wife Mary purchased the Russell grant of land and changed the name to Purcell's Cove, Samuel and his family left Portuguese Cove and to my belief moved to a home on the Halifax Harbour side of Purcell's Cove.

That home was at some time lost to fire.

The next Purcell family home that I know of is pictured in many old photos that feature a white dwelling at the main core of the Cove.

As we all remember Aunt Alice: in front of her little store.
(Ruth Iceton)

Our father, John William, son of Annie Bowman and John George Purcell, himself the grandson of the original Samuel, lived in this home.

Joseph Purcell, brother to John George, lived next door. Joseph was the heir to the land and home where John George lived with his family.

Joseph willed an extensive parcel of land, including the site of his own bachelor home, to our father, John William.

Our dad then built a large home for his family immediately across the road from his uncle, Joseph, as executor to his uncle Joseph's will, then arranged to will the house and land where his father, John George had lived, to Mary Alice Purcell, one of my father's half-sisters.

This home, with its colour changed, still stands today, though a side porch has been removed and a back kitchen added on.

In the meantime, Aunt Alice changed her name to Lyons by marriage, and, following a divorce, then married William Iceton and opened a little store on the premises.

This little store always seemed to be the favourite meeting place of the Cove. Aunt Alice was a very cheerful, energetic person; she was well known for her happy smile and generous hospitality.

Alice was a great-granddaughter of Mary Purcell, known at the time of her death as Mother of the Cove.

Aunt Alice certainly exemplified her grandmother's philosophies.

One of my fondest memories of Aunt Alice was that in her store she had all types of penny candy in large jars. She would have so much patience with us when we wanted to purchase five cents worth of candy and couldn't make up our minds.

One time, in the early 1920s, Aunt Alice became the heroine of the Cove, when there was a terrible storm and the pilot boats and other craft in one part of the cove were in great danger.

In an article in the daily paper reporting the event, it was stated that Alice left the safety of her home to warn the boat owners of the danger.

When big trees uprooted by the force of the gale were crashing to earth, and there was the danger of her falling on the rocks or stumbling into unseen holes, Alice courageously persisted in what she saw as her duty, until she'd warned all the people concerned.

The larger craft lying offshore were piloted to the lee shore of the cove, where the angry seas could do no harm. Two rowboats were lost, but with these exceptions, the fleet escaped harm, thanks to the bravery of Alice Iceton.

Aunt Alice had two daughters, Hilda and Ruth, and Ruth continued living in the family home and helping in the store as long as it was in service to the community.

Following the death of her mother and father, Ruth Iceton still lives in this heritage home. The store is no longer active, but Ruth still has many visitors and still takes a very active part in the news of the Cove.

One of Ruth's prized possessions is an appreciative letter received from President John F. Kennedy for a letter of sympathy Ruthie had sent to him on the death of his infant son in the early 1960s.

The Cove with the little bridge over the brook which runs from Purcell's Pond.

3
Purcell's Cove and Quarries

The Cutting Shed with the top of the Ironstone Quarries in left background. (PANS)

Purcell's Cove

The Quarry Buildings with the mouth of the Northwest Arm in the background.   (PANS)

When Halifax was founded in 1749, many free grants of land in the surrounding areas were given, mostly to ex-servicemen from Britain.

The Quarry lots on the western shore of the Northwest Arm were first granted to Robert Dickey. These lots adjoined land granted to William Russell in the year 1752.

The land grant to Mr. Dickey was escheated; that is to say, it was forfeited through the grantee's failure to produce heirs to take over the land.

Then the Cove quarries were licenced to "the said offices of the commanding Royal Engineers for the use of His Majesty". The British Government's Imperial troops occupied this station for more than 150 years.

With the granite from these quarries, the British Imperial troops built the forts and batteries that surrounded Halifax Harbour for protection from the French and other enemies.

In 1826, a survey map of the north-eastern portion of Purcell's Cove shows a network of roads leading to three quarries: Queen's Quarry, Dalhousie Quarry, and Dominion Quarry.

Probably the first railroad in Nova Scotia, later known as the Trolley Track.   (PANS)

The railroad at the top of the hill.   *(PANS)*

These quarries produced the granite, iron-stone, and slate used in many downtown Halifax buildings, including the historic Town Clock, the walls of the Grand Parade, the old Post Office, and several warehouses on the Halifax water-front.

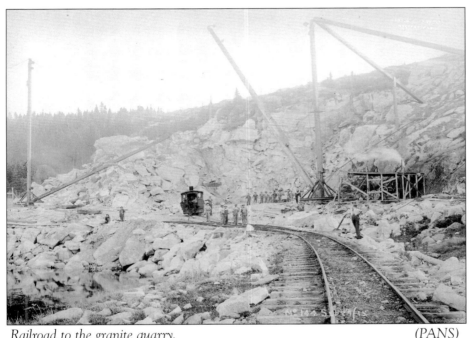

Railroad to the granite quarry.   (PANS)

The major quarry, the one closest to the present main road as you approach the centre of the Cove, appears to be one of the first to be used by the Royal Engineers. In 1834 near this quarry there appeared a new innovation in the province: a railroad. In fact, it could have been the first railroad in Nova Scotia. Six hundred feet of rail were used to bring three ton of stone loaded on one wagon from the quarry at the top of the hill. This railroad, a hundred years later, was known to our generation as the Trolley Track.

Because the first quarry was established very close to the sea at Indian Cove, there was little difficulty getting the granite aboard the barges for delivery to its destination.

However, as more granite was needed, a second quarry was established at a much higher elevation on the granite outcropping, so the railroad was put in to haul the stone from both quarries to the barge at the wharf site.

From earlier times there had been a military wharf built of stone near the granite quarries.

After the railroad was put in use, the wharf was modified and strengthened so the trolley wagons could transfer the large cut stones to ocean barges, to haul to the building sites. There had been another stone wharf near the ironstone quarry on the Northwest Arm across from Point Pleasant Park.

Probably around this time most of the granite from these quarries was used to build the star-shaped Citadel.

The star-shaped Citadel.

Piles of granite slabs at the top of the hill. Note the barren hillside, a result of a forest fire.   (PANS)

Purcell's Cove

Quarry Wharf at Indian Cove.

14   Purcell's Cove

4
Citadel Hill

Entrance to Citadel Hill.
(Vanishing Halifax)

Citadel Hill is one of the most prominent sites in Halifax. When the British founded the city in 1749, they immediately put the British in "British" Canada, by virtue of building the fortification at Citadel Hill.

The building of the Citadel was a calculated act to offset the power of Fort Louisburg in Cape Breton, which had just been returned to the French in 1745.

Lord Cornwallis, sent out to Halifax by the British Crown, reported, "All the officers agree that the harbour is the finest in the world."

Before the stone fortification, however, the Citadel was at first built with pickets, each one ten feet long and six inches thick. At that time there was fear of attack from the Indians. In the meantime the city was growing into a typically British and very civilized city: for example, St. Paul's, the oldest Anglican church in Canada, was opened for service in 1750. It is still standing today on the Grand Parade.

Later on, St. Paul's Parish Hall, built on Argyle Street, used a great deal of ironstone from Purcell's Cove. The stone enjoys the peculiar and beneficial quality of not rusting.

Prior to the noon gun, this "Time Ball" dropped each day. It could be seen from the ships in the harbour; folks could set their timepieces by it.
(PANS)

St. Paul's Church, built on
the Grand Parade.
(Vanishing Halifax)

The Northwest Arm Battery.

(PANS)

Purcell's Cove

Over a period of time, there have been a great number of forts, batteries, redoubts, block houses, barracks, military and naval supply houses built in the Halifax area – more than in any other place in Canada.

The person most responsible for the might of Halifax was a royal duke (who later on fathered Queen Victoria), Prince Edward the Fourth, son of George III. In 1794 he was appointed Commander in Chief of British forces in North America. He first ordered fifteen feet cut off the hill; then, using heavy timbers, a fort was constructed to hold a thousand men and mount enough big artillery to blast any invader out of the harbour. He reinforced all the forts surrounding Halifax Harbour, and he erected a fort at Sandwich Point, later named York Redoubt.

In 1762 a boom had been placed across the Northwest Arm to protect the Citadel on the northwest side. In 1793, another chained boom was placed there attached to a ring bolt on what is now generally called Chain Rock.

Prince Edward was named Duke of Kent in 1799, perhaps for his stalwart work in all the Colonies. But it is said Edward's greatest work was a telegraph system, the first in North America. He hoped he could extend this system as far as Quebec, but it seems to have not operated beyond Nova Scotia.

Edward had taken unto himself a lady-love known as Madame St. Laurent. For her Edward built a large country house with a view of Bedford Basin, near a small pond shaped like a heart. A wooden rotunda was built on the shore of Bedford Basin; it still exists today.

At that time, the first Government House was constructed of a variety of stone from practically every part of the province, including flat stone from Purcell's Cove on the Northwest Arm.

Before the Duke of Kent left Halifax, his final extravagance was the clock tower that stands restored today on the slope of Citadel Hill. The

The first Government House, constructed of stone including stone from the Northwest Arm.

ironstone for the foundation was quarried from Purcell's Cove. In all the ensuing years, this clock has never stopped ticking.

In later years Prince Edward was obliged to put poor Julie aside, marry an authentic princess, and produce an heir to the British throne.

In 1828, the 204 acres of land, including the quarries at Purcell's Cove, was escheated to Gustavus Nichols, a colonel then commanding The Royal Engineers. Colonel Nichols began to rebuild Citadel Hill.

Tens of thousands of tons of squared granite and ironstone were cut from the quarries at Purcell's Cove. This excellent stone was used in the building of this edifice, the twenty-acre, star-shaped fortification, now restored, that almost every visitor to Halifax climbs to inspect. However, what was expected to be accomplished in one year, in total took thirty-three years to complete. Since that time, thousands of ordinary people, as well as such heroes as Wolfe and Churchill, have checked their watches by the noon gun that still booms from the Citadel.

Another Prince Edward, the Prince of Wales, eldest son of Queen Victoria, brought glamour to Halifax in 1860, where a formal ball was held in his honour. The Prince danced with all the prettiest and most important ladies, including the

The Town Clock. (PANS)

Firing the Noon Gun at the Citadel.

Purcell's Cove

Squared granite and iron-stone at Citadel Hill.

Citadel building.

Purcell's Cove

Building the gun entrenchments at Fort Clarence in Point Pleasant Park. (PANS)

Purcell's Cove

daughter of the American consul, who subsequently invited "Mr. Wales" to call on the President.

During the American Civil War, the British figured they had good reason to be prepared. Around 1862, artillery experts rebuilt Fort Ogilvie and Fort Clarence in Point Pleasant Park, installing long-range guns with their far greater accuracy and velocity.

In 1905/06, the British Army garrison was withdrawn and the Royal Naval Dockyard abandoned. A military establishment produced by Ottawa was left in charge to defend Halifax. The British had been in charge for more than one hundred and fifty years.

In future years it was noted that ironstone was obtained at Queen's Quarries for the new Church of England cathedral at Halifax.

Ironstone was obtained from the Queen's Quarry for the new Church of England Cathedral in Halifax. (PANS)

When, prior to the First World War, Germany rose as a threat, Fort Charlotte and York Redoubt were improved and a new battery was installed at Ives Point on McNabs Island.

Even more batteries, with the latest breech-loading and quick-firing guns, were added to McNabs and Sandwich Bluff, formerly known as Spion Kop.

Because of the good fortune of the granite quarries lying so close to the building sites, the construction of the fortifications proceeded with dispatch. Since the initial founding of Halifax, a million fighting men and women, both Imperial and Dominion, have passed through this port into some of the most stirring battles of all times. Yet the fortresses have never taken an enemy blow, or fired a shot in anger.

In the two wars of the first half of the twentieth century, enemy ships approached under water and sank merchant ships within sight of Chebucto Head, but the thunder of Halifax guns remained leashed. So, when the famous Halifax Explosion did come, it was as violent as it was accidental.

One of the guns, still on display at the Citadel.

5
Citadel and Explosion

During the First World War, on December 6, 1917, there was a collision of a French munitions ship, the Mont Blanc, with the Belgian relief freighter the Imo. That collision caused a blast that killed 1,630 people, injured close to 10,000 more, and levelled a square mile of the north end of Halifax. In earlier times many a war had been fought with less carnage.

It has been said that the Citadel Hill had been built so strong it could have received and stopped some of the force of the blast, and so may have saved lives and injuries, as well as preventing a lot of damage on the western side of the hill which lay away from the harbour and explosion.

Wild stories were circulated around Halifax. For instance, "The Germans have attacked us; they have landed at Purcell's Cove."

This was the largest man-made explosion recorded prior to the Atomic Age.

The Halifax Explosion

The greatest man-made explosion prior to the atomic bomb dropped on Hiroshima.

HALIFAX WRECKED
HALIFAX RAVAGÉ

Shaft of the Mount Blanc's anchor hurled two-and-one-quarter miles to land at Edmond's Grounds.

The shaft of the Mont Blanc's anchor was hurled two and one-quarter miles to the wooded shores of the Northwest Arm at the Edmond's Grounds, where it buried itself six feet deep in the earth. Today it can still be seen, close to the spot where it landed.

Our dad, along with one of his sisters, Aunt Alice, went into Halifax to help in any way they could. Dad told us many stories about the explosion, but the one I remember most clearly is the one about Ash Pan Annie.

In my mind was Dad's story about a child who had been saved from the blast by the ash-pan of the stove. Just recently I was fortunate to meet this person who is still known as Ash Pan Annie.

Purcell's Cove

In 1999 I visited Annie Liggins Welsh. I have found she is a niece of an aunt of mine. She herself told me this miraculous story.

Annie, just eighteen months old at the time, lived with her mother and older brother in an apartment on Barrington Street. Her father was serving in the armed forces overseas.

Twenty-six hours after the explosion, Private Benjamin Henneberry, who had lived in the same building as Annie and her family, was searching through the rubble for his own children, who were still missing. He heard a faint cry and, calling for help, began to search for the source of the sound. Under the still-smouldering debris, they found little Annie. She was under the stove, sheltered by an ash-pan, slightly burned but alive. Mr. Henneberry, who had just arrived home from overseas, assumed she was one of his missing girls.

Several days later, Annie was in hospital when she recognized a lady who was just passing through. She called out to the lady, who turned out to be her aunt. The aunt went to the child and then noticed the name on the crib. She said, "That child is not a Henneberry; her name is Annie Liggins."

There is no doubt that, had the toddler not been old enough to recognize this family member, she would have been raised as a Henneberry daughter.

Annie also told me they had never found the bodies of her mother or her brother; she thinks they may have been washed away with the tidal wave that followed the explosion.

This visit with Ash Pan Annie was one of the most rewarding afternoons I have ever spent. Her cheerful character really makes this world a wonderful place to live.

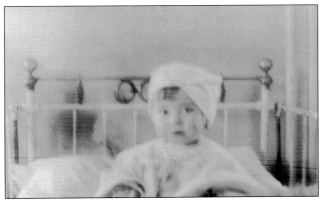

Little Ashpan Annie recovering in hospital

and eighty-some years later.   (Annie Liggins Walsh)

6
The Avalanche

1849 Avalanche in Furgusons Cove

By Alan Ruffman, President, Geomarin

Associates Ltd. with iniative from Peter G. Rogers, Halifax and input from Anjali Vorha of the Public Archives of N.S.

Fearful Consequence of an avalanche.

Those who read of the Alps are familiar with the word avalanche but the thing itself is strange to most who have heard of it. An appalling one was dislodged however, in our neighbourhood at York Redbout, near Fergusons Cove, southward on thursday after- noon, which will be ever memorable in the family who have suffered from the effects. A large mass of ice and snow on the slope of the hill, loosened by the thaw and rain gave way and rushed downwards upon Mr. Thomas Bazoley's house, which was seatted below, burying and wrenching it from the foundation. In the house, an infant in the cradle was smothered to death; an older child was so severly crushed that its recovery can hardly be expected. Mr Bazoley himself received considerable injury, and his wife, advanced in pregnancy, suffered greatly from fright though she fortunately escaped contusion. A girl and lad who happened to be outside were forced by the driving mass into the sea, bu they regained the land; the lad, however, escaped narrowly, having got an arm broken in the scramble for his life. We have gathered these particulars from a hasty interview with Dr. Sawers, who was called to render surgical aid to the sufferers immediately after the disaster occured.

* Avalanche occured on Thursday, March 22, 1849

** With thanks to Peter Rogers sharp eyes who found this original reference while browsing at P.A.N.S.

Artist's drawing of the hill at York Redoubt, near the site of the Avalanche.

7

The Northwest Arm

An early map fixes the name of the inlet on the western side of Halifax as Sandwich River; then the name was changed to Chebucto Bay. The early settlers decided that this lovely sheet of water on the west side of Halifax City be named Northwest Arm, because it was not a river but an arm of Halifax Harbour.

The Arm had always been a mecca of the aborigines for hunting and fishing. It was second nature to them to pick out the most pleasant places to meet; they came from far and wide to camp at the Northwest Arm.

As part of Halifax Harbour, the Arm is also associated with a critical period in British history which led to the settlement of Halifax in 1749. The fate of half a continent was determined by that step.

Using Halifax as a base of operations, Louisburg, in Cape Breton, held by the French, was soon captured. In the following year, Quebec, the French Citadel, also fell.

In 1762, to prevent hostile ships from entering the Arm, a boom had been put in place.

Then, three decades later, in 1793, another chained boom was placed there, attached to a ring bolt on what is now generally called Chain Rock.

The Northwest Arm has been often acknowledged as among the most beautiful spots in the world. Besides that, it is one of the most historic places in Canada.

The Arm is about three miles long and about three-quarters of a mile wide. On the western side of the Arm, the Memorial Tower in Sir Stanford Fleming Park was erected to commemorate the 150th anniversary of representative government in Nova Scotia. This tower is visible still today, from Halifax Harbour, and, like the American Statue of Liberty at Bedloes, proclaims to the world the role of constitutional and responsible government. This historic tower is unique among the world's memorials.

The lower part of the tower being made of native ironstone, the base of native granite, it is

Northwest Arm Memorial Tower built with native stone.

taken for granted that some of this stone came from Purcell's Cove.

The Memorial Tower was opened August 14, 1912 by the Duke of Connaught, son of Queen Victoria.

Hon. Joseph Howe was born at Emscote on the Northwest Arm. On May 1st, 1835 Joseph Howe published an article in his newspaper, The Nova Scotian, critical of Provincial magistrates in Nova Scotia and was tried for libel. Howe defended himself and was acquitted in a landmark case, establishing freedom of the press in Nova Scotia and Canada. Joseph Howe was elected Premier of Nova Scotia in 1860 and Lieutenant Governor of Nova Scotia in 1873.

As a true son of the Arm, he loved to swim, boat, and fish, and his angling proficiency has been recognized by naming a spot at Williams Lake as Howe's Rock.

Another intellectual giant, Sir Charles Tupper, one of the Fathers of Confederation, lived at the Arm. Sir Charles was sworn in as Conservative Prime Minister of Canada in 1896.

The first zoological garden in America was established at Dutch Village, at the head of the Northwest Arm, in 1847, sixteen years before the Central Park collection in New York.

Illuminations at the Arm have been very elaborate: Chinese lanterns, the shores lined with blazing bonfires, and changing lights aided by a brilliant pyrotechnic display. People who have visited other countries have claimed that the Arm illuminations far surpassed anything of the kind they have ever seen abroad. King Carnival annually delighted thousands of visitors at the Northwest Arm; the numerous decorated boats constituted a fairy picture.

I remember one evening in the early 1930s when our dad took us up the Arm in his little motor boat to view a special evening of illuminated floats sponsored by all the businesses in Halifax, Simpsons and Eatons among them. The display was magnificent, like a fairy tale come true. Also, on Aquatic Days at the Arm, we would spend most of the day there, where we would enjoy viewing the swimming and diving displays at the boat clubs. The highlight would be cheering for our young men of the Cove, Louie Purcell and Carl Lynch, as they participated in the shell race. In fact, in 1874 Herring Cove native George Brown was named Champion Oarsman of the World.

Sundays, when there were no races, our dad would take a group of children from the Cove for a boat ride and stop at the Melville Island canteen for an ice-cream, which cost only one nickel at that time.

Regatta Day North West Arm. Halifax. N.S.

(PANS)

Many happy hours have been enjoyed boating and canoeing at the "Dingle" on The Arm.　　(PANS)

Later on, when I was married and living at Melvins, the upper part of the Cove, my husband, our little boy Paul, and I would spend most of Sunday afternoons paddling our canoe up the Arm, stopping at the Dingle Park for an enjoyable picnic lunch. We were often surrounded by a great number of folks, in canoes and other boats, who were also enjoying the beautiful surroundings of the Arm. It is said the best way to see the Northwest Arm is from the water, in a boat or canoe if you have time, but otherwise a motorboat is to be preferred. Make a start near Cobourg Road, coast south as far as Point Pleasant Park, over to Purcell's Cove and, turning about, slowly skirt the western shore of the Arm, up past the historic Memorial Tower at Fleming Park, into Melville Cove, past where the military prison had been, where the Island now is home to the Armdale Yacht Club, then around the head of the Arm and back along the upper eastern shore to the place of beginning.

8
Schools, Churches and Community Halls

The pupils of Falkland Village School in the mid 1930's (Author - fifth from right, second row from back).

In the early days, there was no school at Purcell's Cove. Pupils from the north end attended school in the little village of Jollimore, and the rest of us had to walk about one mile to Ferguson's Cove, to the Falkland Village School. I often wonder if the other pupils of the Cove enjoyed their walk to school; I know I did. I have some very heartfelt memories of this period in my life.

I loved to go to school. Our teacher, Mrs. Gargan, who taught me for the full ten years that I attended Falkland Village School, was simply excellent.

Mrs. Gargan, who taught grades 1 to 10 with between sixty and seventy pupils at the same time in our little one-room schoolhouse, appeared to always have time to treat us as individuals.

Besides the required subjects, she brought into our young lives the arts, including music, poetry, and tap dancing. Also, twice a year, she taught us to perform in a concert which our families greatly enjoyed.

Because we were a large family, at least one of us was present at school each day of the term. For some years we had a black-and-white collie dog named Rover, who accompanied us to school. One year Mrs. Gargan awarded him a prize for perfect attendance.

Rover was allowed to lie beside the pot-bellied stove in the schoolhouse. One day, when the school inspector paid an unexpected visit to our school, Rover was very reluctant to allow him to enter. I suppose he was protecting the pupils from this strange man.

The area including Purcell's and Ferguson's coves was called Falkland, in honour of Lady Falkland, who was the wife of a lieutenant governor of Nova Scotia. Lady Falkland was said to be the daughter of the morganatic alliance of the celebrated Mrs. Jordan and King William IV.

Falkland was a very picturesque village when viewed from Halifax, looking across the harbour. In the early days, the community had two fine churches. When one added the Fortress of York Redoubt standing in for a castle on the summit of a steep hill, this place could well be taken for a scene in the mountains of Spain, given its castle and the village itself overlooking a wide expanse of sea.

The Roman Catholic church, Stella Maris, (*Star of the Sea*) had been built by Irish soldiers stationed at York Redoubt, its cornerstone being laid on August 9, 1845. It was restored in 1976 by local contractor Steve Shaw and co-ordinator Frank Corbett. Its statue, carved in France over two hundred years ago, was rescued from vandalism by Mrs. Demsey and restored by Kenneth Dwyer, a local Purcell's Cove artist.

The Anglican presence goes back well over a hundred years. In Ferguson's Cove an Episcopal church was consecrated on July 27, 1846. The church stood upon a promontory at the entrance to Halifax Harbour near York Redoubt. A large group of Haligonians travelled by steamship to attend the consecration, among them the very prominent Andrew Uniacke who played a part in the services. An offering of 16 pounds was realized.

The chapel was built in the somewhat ornamental Elizabethan style and graced the village for over fifty years.

In later years it was believed most of the Anglicans lived in Purcell's Cove.

This church was dismantled and rebuilt at Purcell's Cove upon a hill on land donated by James Purcell, a descendant of Samuel Purcell, the founder of the Cove.

From the front page of the August 9, 1909 edition of the Evening Mail: "New Anglican chapel opened yesterday at Purcell's Cove. Congregation crowded the building to the doors. Set upon a hill, the church commands a magnificent view of sea and wood, and is visible to every ship which enters the harbour. In the chancel were Rev. Edward Roy and Venerable Archdeacon Armitage."

In 1914 a large forest fire threatened Purcell's Cove. From the Evening Mail, May 26, 1914: "Destruction of church by fire, St. Philip's Church". This fire also destroyed the home of James Purcell, and many other people in the Cove had to go out in their boats for safety.

From the Evening Mail, Wednesday, June 17, 1914: "Purcell's Cove Relief Fund".

It may be taken for granted this fund was towards the building of a new church.

A new St. Philip's Church was built on the same site, a little white church that a number of us will regard with a lot of great memories; it served the parishioners for many years.

St. Philip's Church.   *Longard Collection*

In 1950 there was a need for a new church, and during the construction of the stone church, the little white church was torn down.

On the same site, in 1950, construction of a stone church was undertaken, led by Mr. Velcoff. Says a newspaper of that date: "Board by board, inch by inch, Mr. Evan Velcoff, with Edward Liggins, an accountant, Clarence Soward, a stevedore, and William A. Purcell, a steamfitter, and others, put up the framework."

The amazing thing was that, due to the amount of volunteer labour, the cost of building the entire stone church compared favourably with that of building a rather substantial house at that time.

Much of the furniture that was in use in the little white church was put into use in the new church. The old organ retained its place, as did the pews, now refinished and standing out from the walls. In later years the facade of St. Philips stone church had to be changed for safety reasons.

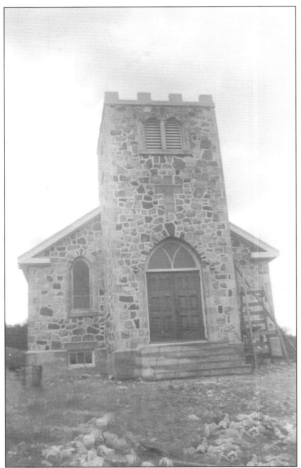

St. Phillip's Church with stone facade . . .

and as it looks today. (Muriel Purcell)

In the mid-1940s the Roman Catholic parishioners felt a need for a church in Purcell's Cove; the members got together and started raising funds for such an effort.

One of the rewarding things of living in a small place like the Cove is the camaraderie among the folks living there. You could see it in how we worked together to raise money for both churches, by mounting one large summer fair, held at the community hall which had been built in 1946.

Another indication of this community co-operation, is that the churches held annual Sunday School picnics at McNab's Island, and all the residents of the Cove were equally welcomed at these outings.

Previous to the opening of St. Cecilia's Roman Catholic Church in 1948, mass was celebrated at the community hall.

It was with great pleasure the community welcomed back Mrs. Gargan, who had taught us at school for so many years. Mrs. Gargan was organist at the community hall masses and then continued to serve in that capacity when St. Cecilia's Church was consecrated in 1948. St. Cecilia's Church was closed in 1973.

St. Cecilia's Church.

The community hall, however, is still going strong, and is now called Purcell's Cove Social Club.

At Dalhousie School, in Purcell's Cove, the first classes for 125 pupils were held in 1942, but the delayed official opening was in 1945. The school was built at a cost of $4,000.00 and finished with volunteer labour from the community. Boys and girls entered the school via separate entrances.

The school closed in 1987; despite the valiant efforts of the Purcell's Cove community to save the building, it was demolished in 1994.

May 22nd, 1820, Lord Dalhousie installed the cornerstone of Dalhousie University on the Grand Parade opposite St. Paul's Church. In 1887, the university was moved to Carlton Street. Some stone was transported from the Parade Ground. In 1923, Stooley Campus was opened.

For a great number of years, Dalhousie University owned a large parcel of land at the north end of Purcell's Cove where Dalhousie School had been built, and across the road where two of the quarries are situated near the Northwest Arm.

Purcell's Cove Social Club.

Dalhousie School

Stone from Purcell's Cove was used for the building of Dalhousie University.

Purcell's Cove

9
Purcell's Ferry

In 1848, a petition for a ferry from Purcell's Cove to Point Pleasant was signed with a large number of names of inhabitants from Herring Cove, Bear Cove, Halibut Bay, Ketch Harbour, and Portuguese Cove. The petition requested a ferry service in order that fishermen could have a clear route to Halifax. Five years following the petition, the regular ferry between Purcell's Cove and Point Pleasant was undertaken in 1853 by Joseph Purcell. A flagpole at Point Pleasant was used to display a signal when a passage was needed. Because mischievous urchins had given false signals on several occasions, a hut was erected at Point Pleasant and a sturdy Irishman, Kennedy by name, was engaged to look after the ferry on the Halifax side. When the ferry was first in operation in 1853, it was largely used for the military authorities, as well as for the workmen and supplies in construction of the surrounding forts and batteries.

On the death of the ferry's founder, his son James was in charge for three years, when he was joined by Robert Cartell, who had married the Widow Purcell. Cartell conducted the ferry in conjunction with James and Samuel Purcell for fifteen years, until 1870, when Major W.A.Purcell, the well-known taxidermist, took up the service until 1900, with his brother taking over the Purcell's Cove portion. Around the year 1900, Robert J. Purcell ran the ferry from Point Pleasant.

At that time, the Park Commission had erected a new ferry house further up the Arm, where there was a more sheltered location for the landing of the boats. Robert's wife, Mary, helped with the running of the ferry for many years.

William Roy Purcell, son of Robert and Mary, left school when he was only twelve years old, taking over the job of helping his father to run the ferry. At that time they still used rowboats, and their fingers became permanently curled up by the rowing.

Over the years, William, better known as Bill, built up the business, having four boats in operation.

This improved service afforded visitors an

Spectacle Island with Ferry House in the background. (George Hebb)

opportunity of enjoying scenic views of rare beauty in the vicinity of Purcell's and Ferguson's coves.

In subsequent years, Bill met his future wife, Theresa. Following their wedding at St. Philip's Church, Purcell's Cove, in 1923, they lived in a home at the Cove that was situated up the hill from the ferry wharf.

Their children were born there, and the older two, Aubrey and Cora, attended Falkland Village School. Aubrey and I were schoolmates and spent a lot of time together when we were young, but I do not think that Aubrey ever learned to swim; at least, he never swam with our friends when we would all go swimming at our wharf.

Purcell's Cove

Bill Purcell

In the early 1940s, Bill moved with his family to Point Pleasant.

For quite a few years, the Purcell family ran a station canteen at the ferry house; it was very popular, if you were just taking a stroll in the park or waiting for the ferry, to stop for a little snack.

There was no bus service to Purcell's Cove until the late 1930s. When we wished to go shopping or go to the movies in the daytime, we would have to take the ferry to Point Pleasant, walk up through the park, and catch the tramcar. In the summer, the rails would come part-way down the park; in winter, we would have to walk to Tower Road and catch the electric tramcar to take us downtown.

The Purcell's Cove Sunday School picnics were always very important events for the Cove people, especially the children. Bill Purcell would always have his large boat prepared to ferry all of us to McNab's Island for a wonderful time, with races and games not only for the children, but also for the adults. The picnic lunches would always be something to look forward to.

Bill said that one year, having kept count, they found they had carried 20,000 passengers. That may have been the year of the Halifax Explosion.

Bill says that, during the early days of World War II, he was rounding Hens and Chickens Shoal (so named because there is one large rock followed by a series of smaller ones) with a ferry-load of sailors. Said Bill, "We saw a submarine coming, and the sailor boys said it did not look like one of ours; the alien must have seen the ferry's red light and thought we were a patrol boat, 'cause she turned around and submerged again." This incident, Bill always claimed, is the very reason why submarine nets had to be laid across the harbour.

Bill's son Aubrey helped him with the ferry service as well as fishing for lobster and tuna. One evening disaster struck, and Aubrey drowned. They had been watching him as he prepared to pull in a lobster trap, and then he disappeared.

That same year, Bill suffered a heart attack. Shortly after this, in 1971, he retired.

The Park Commission decided the ferry house should be demolished and the land made into a picnic place. On this same spot, a plaque has been erected to honour the Purcell family for their more than a century of service to the citizens of Halifax, and in gratitude for the many persons and vessels rescued by them from the waters of the Northwest Arm and Halifax Harbour.

The Purcell Ferry loaded with happy Sunday School picnicers arriving home to The Cove.
(Sheelagh Purcell)

Purcell's Cove

10
The Titanic

On April 14, 1912, the Titanic, at that time the largest ship ever built, was sinking, following a collision with an iceberg in the Atlantic Ocean. The news was so unbelievable, it is no wonder wireless messages became garbled.

It is thought that a ship in the area, the Baltic, sent out a wireless message: Are all Titanic passengers safe? At the same time, another ship, the Asian, sent a message indicating she was towing a disabled ship to Halifax.

The Boston Daily Globe, and many other newspapers, reported that it was the Titanic that was being towed to Halifax with no loss of life.

The authorities at Halifax made huge plans for welcoming the passengers and preparing for their relatives and friends to come to Halifax to meet their loved ones.

Little did those in charge know how drastically those plans would have to be changed.

Just as the newspapers positive reports were being read, the tragic news of the sinking of the Titanic was confirmed.

The steamship Carpathia had received the Titanic's distress call and rushed through the icy waters to the scene of the disaster in hope they would be able to save all the passengers. Later it was found out that another ship, the Californian, had been very close to the Titanic and had seen some of the distress signals, but had misinterpreted them and therefore sailed on.

When the Carpathia arrived at the scene of the disaster, they found some of the lifeboats not filled to capacity, and some with only a few survivors – one with only eight, in fact. All in all, only 705 people survived; 1,523 passengers and crew lost their lives on the ship that had been touted as unsinkable.

The question has often been asked: if there had been more lifeboats, would more lives have been saved? Later on, at the inquiry, it was found that the Titanic was carrying the required number of lifeboats according to the laws of the British Board of Trade. These laws had not been changed for eighteen years.

Also during the inquiry, one of the managers of the White Star Line said he did not think it wise to have lifeboats for everybody because the boat deck would be so crammed that the efficiency of the crew's work would be impaired.

Because of such testimony following the disaster, there was a change made, in that all ships must carry enough lifeboats to accommodate all persons aboard.

Neither at the American nor the British inquiries were formal charges laid, but a bold assertion was made: All the lives may have been saved, but for the negligent indifference of the Californian to the Titanic's signals.

One specific accusation against those in charge was that of overconfidence that the ship would not sink.

Another court report stated that the loss of the Titanic was due to a collision with an iceberg brought about by the excessive speed at which the ship was being navigated.

Another point, made in evidence given before the Senatorial Commission in the American inquiry, was that there had not been any boat drill or station practice; also, no general alarm was given; neither was there in place an organized system for securing the safety of those on board.

In the meantime, Halifax became a city in mourning; church bells pealed for the dead, and black bunting was a common feature. Instead of welcoming passengers, Halifax therefore had the grim task of sending out a steam-driven cable ship, MacKay Bennett, to search for bodies and return the remains to Halifax for identification.

On April 26, the MacKay Bennett, the death ship, returned to Halifax. On her return, she passed by the wharf where she usually docked and made her way up the harbour to the naval dockyard. A place was needed to provide security from the news photographers and curious people. Those in charge chose the dockyard because of its high wall which, I am told, was built from iron-stone from Purcell's Cove.

Besides the height of this wall, a detail of men from the navy kept the curious onlookers from viewing the gruesome sight.

While church bells rang, the bodies of the deceased were carried by stretchers from the ship to horse-drawn hearses. The Mayflower Curling Rink was used as a morgue to accept the bodies and to prepare for the grief-stricken relatives to come and identify the bodies of their loved ones.

Of the 209 bodies brought to Halifax, 59 were

Gate of the Dockyard and wall built from ironstone from the quarries at Purcell's Cove. (PANS)

identified and shipped to other places for burial; it was believed that 150 victims would remain in Halifax forever.

One of the first services for some of the unknown victims was conducted at St.Mary's Roman Catholic Church, now St.Mary's Basilica. (It may be noted in passing that the facade of the beautiful church features stone from a quarry at Purcell's Cove.)

Following this service, the unidentified bodies were buried at Mount Olivet Cemetery.

A funeral for fifty of the Titanic's victims was held at the Brunswick Street Methodist Church. The theme of the eulogy, was that the unknown dead would never be forgotten, that their graves would be kept forever as fresh reminders of an unnecessary loss of life.

This group was taken to Fairview Lawn Cemetery. One graveyard eulogy suggested, "They shall rest quietly in our midst under the murmuring pines and hemlocks, but their story shall be told to our children and our children's children."

The graves, now all with headstones of native stone, are formed in the shape of the bow of a ship and face northeast. Decades later, it was found that the bow of the wreck of the Titanic was facing the same way.

At the Fairview Lawn Cemetary, the gravestones of the Titanic victims were arranged in the shape of the bow of a ship.

Purcell's Cove

At another church, St. George's, often called the Round Church, the congregation prayed for a little two-year-old boy, at first known as the Unknown Child of Titanic. This little boy's body was recovered by the crew of the MacKay Bennett. Many of the crew attended the funeral, and the crew later had a headstone erected to the boy's memory. Later on, it was discovered that the lad's name was Gösta Pálson, the son of one Alma Pálson, who had, as it happened, been buried very close to her son's grave.

Titanic's Canada-bound passengers and crew numbered approximately 120 persons. Around 40 of these passengers, plus two crew members, survived the sinking.

One of the lost passengers was Charles Melville Hays, president of the Grand Trunk Railway, which later became Canadian National Railway. Mr. and Mrs.Hays were residents of Montreal and had been guests of the White Star Line on the maiden voyage of the Titanic. Mrs. Hays survived the disaster.

Harry Markland Molson, a member of the well-known brewing family, was the richest Canadian aboard. Having, during his lifetime, swum away from two previous shipwrecks, he unfortunately did not survive this one.

One Haligonian, George Wright, of Wright's World Business Directories and a prominent construction contractor, born in Tuft's Cove, Nova Scotia, is reported (by the Public Archives of Nova Scotia) to have been among the casualties simply because he slept through the entire disaster. If so, this might have been a direct result of the lack of a general alarm. Wright seems to have had a considerable conscience, for he was committed among other things to better housing for the working poor, and had built a housing development in Halifax integrating homes for the rich and poor.

My personal memory goes back to cable ships: one day, when I had first met my future husband, we were aboard the Dartmouth ferry, which operates between Halifax and Dartmouth. We observed a cable ship, and he told me that his father had been a crew member on that cable ship for a number of years, and that he also had been working there just before the Second World War began; he then enlisted in the army.

But at that time, neither of us had known that these cable ships, twenty years earlier, had been known as death ships, because they had been handed the grim task of recovering the bodies of the passengers of the ill-fated Titanic.

11
Memories of Cove and Island

Purcell's Cove as a whole had always been well-known as a favourite spot for boating and picnicking, not just for locals, but for Halifax residents as well. The picturesque little cove was protected by a small island, Spectacle Island.

The island was blessed with a large number of grassy spots that were very suitable for holding picnics.

Also, in the early days, many of the young folks would visit the cove for some amateur mountain-climbing. The quarry situated close to the road was their favourite spot. At the present time, that whole area has changed because of the great amount of foliage that has grown up around the quarry.

Boating at The Cove.

Picnic on Spectacle Island at the turn of the 19th century.　　　　*Phyllis Fenerty*

As well, at that time, the area was very popular for picking blueberries. They used to grow in great abundance around the granite mounds. Now the thickened growth of trees appears to have almost obliterated the young berry bushes that used to be so fruitful.

With the change in lifestyle nowadays, very few people take the time to go picking berries.

Oh, what endearing memories we have of enjoying a blueberry pie made with fresh berries that we had picked with our own hands!

Growing up in the Cove, one of our main recreation sports was swimming, and our family's large wharf was the general meeting place for all

John William Purcell's Wharf close to the island.

Spectacle Island.

of our friends for this activity.

We spent many wonderful days just playing or boating in this area.

We grew up loving the water. A family tale tells about the time when I was just a toddler and fell off the wharf. The brother with me had to pelt up the hill and across the road for help. It is said I was not at all afraid of the water, and that I just kept moving my arms and my legs and kept afloat until help arrived.

I suppose most children raised by the sea are natural water babies, while those raised in cities, without the natural knowledge and love of the water, tend often to fear it, with the result that, without appropriate swimming lessons, this translates to an inability to allow the body to float naturally in water.

In fact, I've heard stories about shipwrecked sailors being saved, in their estimation because they had, as children, learned to swim and have no fear of the water.

For example, some men who were passengers on the ill-fated Titanic and had jumped or been thrown into the sea, had swum away from the sinking ship and reached the safety of the lifeboats.

We water babies felt it such an achievement to learn we could swim all the way from Purcell's Cove to Spectacle Island, so named because of the two rounded mounds which some saw as the lenses in a pair of eye-glasses.

This little island had become a very important memento in our lives. Our visits to the island, whether for picnics, weiner roasts, or just exploration, provided us with very happy memories. One of these memories which stays very close to me is when we young folk of the Cove were planning a weiner roast on the island.

We spent a busy day in preparation for this outing. We used our father's large dory to take firewood to the island for our planned bonfire, which always seemed to be the highlight of the evening.

The dory, used to transport the Gang over to the island, we had hauled safely up on the beach, or so we thought.

We were thoroughly enjoying our evening. Following roasting of the wieners, we were sitting around the bonfire, singing some of our favourite songs, when all of a sudden I was devastated to see that the tide had come in and there was Dad's dory drifting slowly out to the open harbour. Thankfully the water was calm that night, with no wind.

I was so worried because my dad was one of those outstanding fathers who would always trust us without question, and, up to that time, I don't think I had ever disappointed him.

We ran to the lee side of the island and looked across the water for a light or other signs of life. But the Cove people appeared to have settled down for the night.

We shouted for assistance; thankfully, my older sister Doris had just arrived home, and had come down to our wharf to check to see what was going on. She answered our distress call, borrowed a boat from our cousin, rowed out to the harbour, and rescued the dory, thus providing a happy ending.

A most unhappy ending for many was the crash of the German airship Hindenburg in 1937. I remember on July 4, 1936 as we stood on our wharf at the cove, we observed the Hindenburg as it cruised slowly over Halifax on its scheduled flight to New York, probably taking photos of all the harbour defenses. Little did we know at that time of the oncoming war with Germany.

Memories of watching the Hindenburg are very vivid. Oh, to have owned a camera at that time, to record a bit of history, especially when we heard, later on, of its tragic end when it burst into flames while attempting to land in New Jersey, with a loss of 37 lives.

There is a small lake, at the back of the Cove, which has always been known as Purcell's Pond. Some of the young folk used to swim there in our day. Our father used to forbid us to go swimming there, because he felt the water was not as pure as that in the cove.

We were very fortunate to live in that era before pollution.

Now at times the water in the cove is unfit to swim in, while Purcell's Pond is still safe and is the favourite swimming place for most of the young people in the Cove.

The cove was not only great as a recreation spot for the summertime, but during the winter the cove water would freeze over; we spent many wonderful days skating there.

Also, Purcell's Pond supplied us with many days of enjoyable skating. When it snowed we would go and shovel the snow off the ice to prepare for some competitive hockey games.

There were very few indoor rinks. The Northwest Arm League began with the teams playing on outdoor ponds and lakes.

This is probably what makes playing hockey Canada's favourite game.

Also at that time the Trolley Track would be a good straight incline for some amateur attempts to learn to ski.

Now, with all the heavy undergrowth, it is almost impossible to find the original Track.

At present, with the almost steady stream of automobiles travelling through Purcell's Cove, it would probably be difficult for folks living there now to realize that during our generation, in the evenings, we could use the road to go sleighing. We could start at the top of the hill, by the church, and enjoy a thrilling ride down to the little hill at Louie Purcell's. There were very few automobiles travelling the road at that time.

On January 21, 1954, an article in the Halifax Mail Star discussed the ownership of Spectacle Island.

Wintertime at Purcell's Cove.

"Almost within a stone's throw of the shore, the island is composed of two sugar-loaf mounds rising from the water and joined by a narrow neck of land. Because of its shape, which has a resemblance to a pair of eyeglasses, as has been mentioned, the name Spectacle was bestowed on it many years ago by some people possessed of imagination.

Tales of supposed buried treasure cached below the earth of its surface have led at times to digging operations, although details seem to have been lost concerning just what is supposed to have led treasure-seekers to the site.

Within memories of people still living at the Cove are images of deep holes being dug by treasure-seekers in the narrow strip of land linking the two hills of Spectacle Island. Those who were drawn to the island by tales of treasure were said to have been people from the nearby city and surrounding area."

At that time, it was stated in the newspaper article that the island did not appear on the county assessment rolls.

Deeds show that, when Samuel Purcell, in 1828, purchased the 200-acre parcel of land from the Pernettes, heirs of William Russell, that parcel included the little island.

In 1852, Samuel Purcell divided the ownership of this land between four of his sons: Samuel, Joseph, Benjamin, and James. In each of these deeds he left one-quarter of the island to each son.

Following other land deals with his brothers, James could have become owner of a total of one-third of the island, because he was the only brother who included the one-third ownership in further deeds passed down.

At the present time, Edward Liggins, a descendant of the first Samuel Purcell, is on the assessment rolls as the owner of one-third of the island, and is paying taxes on same.

12
Purcell's Cove Quarries

My personal memories so often go back to the quarries and the wonderful times we experienced at these places. At the top of the hill, the Engineers' Quarry, one of the most picturesque, was left in the early 1930s as an almost sheer wall of beautiful granite, with a pool of pristine, clear water at the base.

This granite wall had many little niches and indentations which created footways to and from which we children could do some rather dramatic mountain-climbing, at least in our opinion.

When we would go blueberry-picking near this place, and got hot and tired, we found it so refreshing to sit and dangle our feet in the cool, clear water.

Occasionally the boys would go skinny-dipping. One day when the boys were enjoying just such a refreshing dip, a group of us girls came to the top of the cliff and surprised them. We threw over some dried leaves, and when the boys looked up, they thought that there were rocks coming down. Did they scatter for safety!

This quarry was also a favourite place to hold our corn boils and weiner roasts.

Near this quarry, there is a large rocking stone deposited there by the retreating glaciers of the last Ice Age. We climbed on this rock many times. At the present time it is difficult to find because of the many trees that have grown around the stone.

On the other side of the road, near the Northwest Arm, were two ironstone quarries, where the stones were a rusty colour.

At the base of this cliff was a swampy area where a little dam had been built to hold the water in. When winter came, it would freeze over and make the most splendid rink for skating and playing hockey. It was justly named the Bog.

Almost surrounded by cliffs, it would help to protect us from the cold winds coming in from the harbour.

Some of the young people who learned to skate there had good hockey careers playing in the Northwest Arm League. In fact, one of my

Left background shows the side of the Engineers' Quarry which had the pool at the bottom.   (PANS)

Purcell's Cove   53

The Rocking Stone with a view of Purcell's Pond peeking out at left.   Longard Collection

Purcell's Cove

The ironstone quary close to the Northwest Arm. PANS

brothers, Walter Purcell, played hockey with the famous Turk Broda of the Toronto Maple Leafs when they were serving in the army overseas.

One of Walter's nephews, Walter Butch MacLean, tried out for the Toronto team, but this was before the Expansion League, when very few players were needed. Unable to play for the Maple Leafs, Walter went professional with the New Jersey Devils.

While we were enjoying all those happy times, little did we think of the historical part that these quarries played in the history of the Cove.

The quarry on Bluestone Road now known as "The Bog".

The large quarry closest to the road as you approach the centre of the Cove appears to have been one of the first to be used by the Royal Engineers.

Memories remain of a very large dynamite blast at this quarry on August 1, 1931, after which a huge amount of stone tumbled down and covered the road; some large boulders actually landed in the shore-waters.

For a time the road was, of course, impassable, and that very day there was a funeral for Mrs. Umlah, and so the procession had to go the long way around, through Spryfield down to Herring Cove and then to Purcell's Cove, adding probably ten miles or more to the route.

In 1957 these large stones, some weighing from one to fourteen tons, along with sixteen thousand tons of jagged granite quarried from the top of the hill which backs the cove, were taken to their ultimate destination on McNab's Island. When the tons of stone were quarried, the granite hill was reduced; what was previously a favourite watering hole disappeared entirely, and along with it went a lot of nostalgic memories. Some days fifty tons of granite were moved by truck to the Cove's shore, where it was hoisted aboard barges and moved to its new site. There it was used to build a safeguard to help protect the neck of land that jutted out into the harbour, at the tip of which Mauger's Beach Lighthouse stands.

On the shore of the Northwest Arm, across from the ironstone quarries, was the site of the old Provincial Penitentiary, which was built of ironstone from this quarry.

It is said that, in later years, the stone from this demolished penitentiary helped to build the nearby St. Mary's University.

The quality of the stone has always been appreciated by builders, as one of them, in a report dated somewhere between 1817 and 1826, noted, "I had recourse of a very fine granite from a quarry on the Northwest Arm." He was quite impressed by the very hard nature of the stone.

13
McNab's Island & Maugers Beach Lighthouse

McNab's Island was first called Cornwallis Island, named for Colonel Edward Cornwallis, the founder of Halifax.

One of the guardians of Halifax Harbour was the Sherbrooke Tower, built from granite from Queen's Quarry, known for its fine quality. This tower was built at Mauger's Beach as a defence fortification for Halifax. A lighthouse was built on top of the tower and completed in 1828. For many years this light was a beacon for all the ships that entered Halifax Harbour, as well as for the local fishermen.

Mauger's Beach features a stretch of land which juts out into the harbour from the west side of McNab's Island.

Just before World War II, a new lighthouse was built on this site to replace the Sherbrooke Tower, which had deteriorated.

During the time of World War II, there was fear of enemy submarines entering Halifax Harbour. To prevent this, and to guard the outbound convoys which gathered in Bedford Basin,

Sherbrooke Tower, built with granite from Purcell's Cove.

an anti-submarine net was placed across Halifax Harbour from the shores of York Redoubt to Mauger's Beach Lighthouse.

The contrast between the shorelines on each side of the harbour is unique. On the cove side of the harbour, the shoreline is very rocky, extending miles out to sea. On the McNab's Island side, it is noted for outstanding sandy beaches.

Lighthouse at Mauger's Beach showing anti-submarine net, 1943. (National Archives of Canada)

Of course, McNab's was a favourite spot for all our picnics, both family and community. The island is almost surrounded by sandy beaches; when the tide is out, there is a panoramic view of firmly packed sand.

On our picnics, we played very amateurish ball games on this expanse of beach. From the oldest to the youngest, picnickers enjoyed a good, rousing game. Some of the players were so young they could hardly hold a bat. The camaraderie was so enjoyable. The memories are still very precious to me.

Besides enjoying very tempting picnic lunches, we would also take pleasure in picking the raspberries and blackberries which grew in such great abundance on the island.

When World War II had been declared, my brother Walter and several boys from the Cove were called to serve in the army militia. They were stationed at Fort McNab on McNab's Island.

Previous to the declaration of war, the boys had lied about their ages and joined the army militia just for something to do, and to make a little extra money.

The forts at that time were unprepared to house the young men properly. For one thing, there was a shortage of cooks to prepare good food for their young appetites.

So, with the boys there, where did the girls go? Every Sunday we would ask the ferryman, Bill Purcell, to take us over to McNab's Island to see them and take extra food for them. On one of our visits, we were a little early, so we had time to spare before the boys could get leave to come to meet us.

We decided we would go for a tour and visit the lighthouse. While we were walking out along the long stretch of land, the sky turned dark. Just then, what appeared to be a tornado struck the lighthouse area. A small boat was picked up by the gale and smashed against the rocks. We had just reached the protection of the lighthouse when a heavy rain of hailstones, as large as golf balls, broke every window in the vicinity, including those in the home of the lighthouse-keeper.

As with many tornadoes, this was followed by many hours of torrential rain.

Meanwhile, my brother Walter had been on lookout duty at the Fort. He had been watching us as we were walking out on this stretch of land, and he became very alarmed when the storm struck, because he lost track of us. He had started to leave the Fort when an officer stopped him. Walter explained that he just had to go because he was so worried that his sister and friends could have been injured by the storm.

In the meantime, from the lighthouse area, we could see my cousin Bill coming in his boat to pick us up at the military wharf. We slogged through the pouring rain to meet the boat, while, at the same time, Walter arrived at the wharf. When he saw that we were all safe, he stood stock-still and exclaimed, "Thank God!"

Halifax escaped this storm.

When we arrived home, we found many houses had had their roofs damaged by the hailstones. In fact, my sister-in-law was walking around our large kitchen with an umbrella over her head to protect her from the heavy drips.

Somewhere down the line, when the military authorities found out the real age of our local boys, they gave them honourable discharges. In that same year, one of these fine lads, Dougald Gargan, died as a result of suffering from the dread disease diabetes.

Later on, my brother Walter and his friend Bobby Gilfoy rejoined the army and served their country overseas.

Donald White joined the Royal Canadian Navy; unfortunately, Donald's life was lost when he was a member of the crew of HMCS Fraser, which was lost in action in the Bay of Biscay.

Later on, in the last days of the war, my brother-in-law Charlie and his family looked after the lighthouse at Meager's Beach for one summer.

One sunny day, when my husband and I and our little boy were spending a weekend there, we had a very enjoyable time swimming and playing on the sandy beach. The men went fishing and caught a large halibut, which made such a tasty dinner with fresh raspberries for dessert.

That night the fog came in, and the noise from the foghorn was deafening. In all my life, I just could not believe that a sound could be so tremendously loud.

Back home at the Cove, the foghorn was simply a distant, rather pleasant reminder that ships were being kept safe, but, from that night on, I realized how brave the lighthouse-keepers and their families are.

At one time there was a tale told about a lighthouse keeper in charge of the Mauger's Beach lighthouse. One day he travelled across the harbour to Herring Cove to cut a Christmas tree. He had an accident and injured one of his legs; unfortunately, this leg had to be amputated and was buried at Herring Cove.

Some time later he returned to his lighthouse duties.

So goes the tale, of all the ships that sailed in and out of Halifax Harbour at that time: They sailed between a man's legs.

A submarine cruising by Mauger's Beach Lighthouse.

Purcell's Cove

14
World War II

York Redoubt defending Halifax Harbour.

In September, 1939, when Canada declared war on Germany, like the rest of our allies we were greatly unprepared. Most of the fortifications around Halifax and along the coast from Purcell's Cove had been left in ill-repair.

They suddenly had to be brought up to standard and be made habitable, in order to house the thousands of young men who had volunteered to fight for their country. Prior to the war, the area had seen other uses.

Fort Connaught, situated between Purcell's Cove and Ferguson's Cove, had not been manned between wars.

Because of the overabundance of rocky areas in our Cove, there was no field or flat area large enough to play a ball game. We used the large field in Fort Connaught for practice and played some games there.

We also used the fort as a short-cut to walk through to school.

A little further along the coast, York Redoubt had been better cared for, so we got permission from the sergeant major to play league games there. One game played at York Redoubt appeared to be a Purcell family affair. My two older brothers, Roland and Bill, were players on the team; younger brother Walter was bat boy. One of the oldest sisters of the family kept score, the game was umpired by another sister, while I was just an ordinary cheerleader and spectator. At one of these games, I had been called C.H.N.S. by the opposition. C.H.N.S. was the name of one of the local radio stations.

Sandwich Battery was better preserved because it was one of the last forts constructed. The guns of this battery commanded the approach to Halifax Harbour.

Once the forts were manned for war, the soldier-trainees naturally looked for some socializing, a place to visit when they were on leave. So the lives of the residents of Purcell's Cove greatly changed as these young soldiers were welcomed warmly into local homes.

The Royal Engineers had been the British force responsible for building the first Halifax fortifications. In a way, it was history repeating itself, for the first soldiers that were stationed at Fort Connaught were the Royal Canadian Engineers.

Some of these army lads that came from across Canada, especially those from the Prairies, were quite taken with the dramatic coastal scenery. Some of these young lads had never seen the sea, or had a chance to be in a boat or on a ship. Some people of the Cove happily introduced some of the fellows to boating, as well as showing them great hospitality.

Our home, with our large family, was often like a bee-hive. Almost every hour of the day and evening, it seemed, someone was always dropping in for a visit. Most evenings, our large kitchen table was crowded with a group of our friends playing card games. When my brother Walter was serving overseas in World War II, our dad made a point of welcoming the young lads serving in the Forces near our home.

At times our home appeared more like a hostel.

Perhaps the most hospitable person was Alice

Purcell Iceton, who ran Iceton's Store. Aunt Alice's store was known as the general meeting place of the community, so, of course, it was the most popular place for the servicemen to meet and spend their spare time.

Aunt Alice was so kind and friendly. In fact, she often acted as a second mother to them.

The Cove had no suitable place to supply entertainment for the troops. A group of us girls got together to try to solve the problem.

We asked my dad, who was one of the school trustees, for permission to hold dances in the schoolhouse.

On Saturdays we would go up to Fort Connaught and ask the commanding officer if he could send a detail of soldiers with us to go to the schoolhouse to move all the desks out to the porch, so we could have lots of room for dancing.

The servicemen had wonderful times at the dances. The only problem was a shortage of girls. The tag dances were the most popular (and much in demand). Tag dances give permission to break in and dance with a girl already partnered; then, after a short time, another man is eligible to do the same.

On Sundays, the soldiers would come and return the desks to their places to prepare for school on Monday.

When we were unable to obtain a local band to play for the dances, the servicemen supplied their own musicians.

Actually, the dances became so popular that the young recruits from the Royal Canadian Artillery from the other forts, would come, too, and have a good time.

These dances were so much appreciated by the boys, and we had no problems. There was no drinking or drugs; no one was interested in fighting each other, for they, as a brotherhood, were being prepared to go fight the enemy. Their outlet was to simply have a good and innocent time.

It was during this time that many of the girls from the Cove met their future husbands. I was one of those girls.

One evening, I walked into Iceton's Store and saw this soldier standing there. I had seen hundreds of soldiers by this time, but for this one my heart skipped a couple of beats and I said, "That is the one for me." Luckily, as it turned out, he felt the same way. He was one of the first soldiers I'd seen in the new battle-dress uniform with the wedge cap. Oh, he was so handsome!

Previous to this, the recruits wore a more formal jacket with knee-breeches and the cumbersome puttees, often so detested by those forced to wear them.

Larry not only fell in love with me but also with the Cove.

Larry was from Dartmouth; he was an only child whose mother doted on him. When he came to our home, however, he revelled in becoming part of a large family where everyone worked and shared. Our family became his family and Purcell's Cove became his true home. The Cove was his favourite place to hunt and fish; the paths back to Purcell's Pond and up to the granite quarries were almost an everyday stroll. I was so happy to find someone who enjoyed the outings to the memorable places so dear to me.

There was one event in 1942 that brought the disaster of war close to Nova Scotia, the rest of Canada, and especially Newfoundland. In fact it had been noted as the most dramatic event of the war on Canadian soil. During the first years of the war, from 1939 to 1941, the German submarines had stayed away from the Gulf of St. Lawrence and the American coast because of the fear that attacking an American ship could anger the Americans and cause them to enter the war.

Following Pearl Harbour, the Battle of the Atlantic and Gulf of St. Lawrence took on a greater role. The Germans tried to stop the large amount of supplies being transported to Britain. Several allied ships had been sunk by German submarines.

On October 13, 1942, the Newfoundland car ferry, the Caribou, sailed on its regular service from North Sydney, Nova Scotia to Newfoundland, accompanied by a mine-sweeper whose job it was to protect the ferry from enemy submarines. During that fateful night, the Caribou was sunk by a torpedo from a German submarine, The Laughing Cow.

Purcell's Cove.
Dec. 4th 1941.

Receipt in full on payment of a parcel of land.
To Mrs Belfountain of Purcell's Cove.
Bought of Mrs R. Purcell, also Purcell's Cove,
The land measuring Fifty by Eighty feet.
Thank you.
Mrs W. Shano,
Per. Mrs R. Purcell,

Receipt, which served as a deed, received on the purchase of a lot of land just following the marriage of Elsie Purcell to Larry Bellefontaine.

Unfortunately, some of the lifeboats on the Caribou were also damaged by the torpedo. There was a large loss of life: 136 men, women, and children.

A Purcell's Cove couple, Mr. and Mrs. Peter Hicks, had been booked to sail on the Caribou that evening. The story I have been told is that Mr. Hicks had just lost track of the time, and when Mrs. Hicks found him, they hailed a taxi to take them to the dock. The taxi driver informed them the Caribou had just sailed out of the harbour.

Later on during the war the 18th Anti-Airfcraft Battery, built with dummy guns, was entrenched at the northwest end of the Cove, situated near the granite quarry area. This battery, despite being incapable of replying to alien fire, was placed there to help protect Halifax from attacks by air. Such dummies, common also in Britain, were devised because there was simply not enough time or materials to build the real McCoy.

During the war, in the military tradition of the long and costly wars in Europe, Halifax had repaired 7,000 ships and sent 17,593 vessels out in convoys, protected by a Canadian Navy that had swelled to four hundred ships.

The convoys formed in Bedford Basin; when they sailed out of Halifax Harbour, we had a very clear view of all the ships from the Cove. We would often row our little boats out the harbour and wave farewell to our brave fighting men en route to the fighting zones.

These troop ships were so impressive. The Aquatania, the Empresses of Britain and Australia, the 85,000 ton Queen Elizabeth and her companion Queen Mary carried as many as 15,000 troops each. But time takes its toll, and most of them are no longer in service. However, the Queen Mary at the present time is anchored at Los Angeles, redecorated and used as a floating hotel.

The gracious Queen Mary as she steams out of Halifax Harbour.

With the large amount of shipping going in and out of Halifax Harbour, sometimes laden with explosives; with the magazine at Burnside; the huge stores at Imperial Oil; and with the memory of the Halifax Explosion during the last war, it made it very fearful for Haligonians.

One April night in 1942, we were awakened by large cannon-like noises. My husband had been on leave; he was serving in the 23rd Royal Canadian Artillery Battery at Fort Sandwich. Thinking it was the artillery guns firing from his station, he ran all the way back to the fort. Later we found out that the Navy was firing its guns at the Allied steamship Trongate, which carried a large quantity of explosives on board. A fire had broken out which they were unable to put out. The Navy decided to sink the ship to prevent another explosion.

With the influx of all the armed forces into Halifax together with almost all their families, the city became severely overcrowded. The people of Halifax tried to show the great hospitality for which they have become known, but it was impossible to do under these conditions.

We found it very crowded in the little place we were renting, but we still made room for a friend of my husband's to be able to bring his wife out from Calgary.

Rationing of food was unique. I used to have to catch the early morning bus to go into Halifax, and would have to stand in line to be able to buy a half-pound of butter. Margarine was unavailable at that time.

From being in such close proximity to a lot of happenings in the war effort, we were so happy to hear the great news on that triumphant day in May, 1945 when the Allied victory in Europe was complete. All through Canada it was a day of celebrations.

I was so proud to attend a victory celebration at the garrison grounds on the western side of

Citadel Hill, but while we were celebrating, little did we know that there was a riot being organized on the other side of the Hill.

So many servicemen, along with their families, had been crowded into the city. The overcrowded lodgings, high rents, scant supplies, to say nothing of over-burdened laundries at the really basic level of necessities, naturally caused a good deal of disgruntlement.

Of course, local people suffered also from this over-crowding forced upon them by wartime conditions, but a lid was kept on the pressure boiler both by locals and servicepeople, because there was a war to be won.

However, on V.E. Day, the lid came off. Unwisely, as it happens, the local authorities had decreed that the liquor outlets be closed. As a consequence, a large number of the unhappy service people did not have access to a party mood way of finally expressing their pent-up frustrations.

The mob bombarded the liquor stores, broke in, got what they were after, fuelled up and decided to take the town apart.

And by the headlines of the local paper, that is just what they did.

Most of the businesses were badly damaged and looted; as a news report stated, sections of blitzed London could not have looked worse than the Halifax business section following the riot.

While this was going on, thousands of other service people left the disturbance for the peaceful parts of the city.

A special commission appointed by the federal government eventually placed the primary blame for the riot on Navy personnel. The owners of the damaged and looted premises throughout the business core received full compensation from the federal treasury.

Near the end of the war, on July 18, 1945, a second explosion again created havoc in Halifax. About 6:30 in the evening, there was a sound like a gigantic thunder-clap, and a large mushroom cloud appeared over the magazine at Burnside on the Bedford Basin at the upper end of Halifax Harbour.

At that time the magazine probably had enough ammunition stored there to level the cities of Halifax and Dartmouth.

An ammunition barge had blown up, which caused continuous explosions for 24 hours. A succession of detonations was punctuated frequently by roaring blasts of ever-increasing, vivid sheets of flame, lurid and awesome.

It was only a little over two months since the V.E. Day riots. This time the Navy personnel became heroes; they knew the danger they faced, but they still volunteered to stay and help the magazine staff to fight the raging fires, while dodging a rain of

debris and five-inch shells whizzing by their heads, never knowing when another blast would occur.

Fortunately there were only a few casualties and only one death during the initial blast. Some ships previously anchored in Bedford Basin sailed out and then anchored in the Northwest Arm.

No one slept in the greater Halifax area that night; thousands were evacuated from the city and the communities that ring the inner harbour. A large number of evacuees came to Purcell's Cove, some simply because they'd heard tales of the Great Explosion that had levelled the north end of Halifax in 1917.

The residents of the Cove readily welcomed these families, some with infant children. Just to demonstrate how danger so often confuses the mind, in some cases the families, especially the ones that came to our family's home, had come provided

Mushroom cloud from the magazine explosion; photo taken from Purcell's Cove.   *(PANS)*

with everything but diapers. Fortunately my older sister, who was living in the family home at the time, had two infants of her own.

So, on the following day, when I went to help, I certainly put in my share of diaper laundry. What I remember most about such a mundane chore was the pleasure of hanging diapers outside in a lovely breeze on a warm sunshiny day.

When we ran out of fresh food, the men simply went out fishing, and the families really enjoyed a nice, fresh, fish dinner.

We were greatly relieved and thankful when we heard the all-clear news and knew that these families could return safely to their homes.

On August 14, 1945, Japan surrendered; at last the long war came to an end. This time the celebrations were peaceful and orderly. As the old saying goes, A lesson well learned.

Granite from The Cove was used in the statue of Robert Burns.

15
Summer People Living in the Cove

Many well-known people from Halifax lived in their bungalows at the Cove during the summer months.

In the early years, Rev. Armitage, Archdeacon, and his family spent many happy summers there.

The famous painter W.E. DeGarthe, when he was a young man, spent a great deal of time visiting the Cove, where he enjoyed many hours at one of his favourite pastimes, fishing. DeGarthe's paintings of the sea became world-famous. He was buried at Peggy's Cove, and his grave is surrounded by carvings in the granite stone there, which feature topics of fishermen and the sea. A gallery is still open there, where his paintings of the sea are for sale.

Many of us have fond memories of his visits; at that time, we had no idea he would become so famous.

The photos taken by Wm. MacAskill have also become world-famous. Most of his photos are of the sea. Mr. MacAskill had a house built at Ferguson's Cove in the shape of a ship.

During the Second World War, a major in the army and his wife spent an enjoyable summer living in one of these bungalows at Metchler's Point. I had a summer job at this place, mostly to keep the major's wife company while he was away.

They had no children; the love of their lives was a beautiful russet Irish setter named Mickey. Part of my job was to take Mickey for walks; when the owners were both away, I took care of Mickey completely. We spent many wonderful days hiking through the woods and over the hills up near the quarries at the back of the Cove. Mickey became very attached to me.

When winter came, the major and his wife moved to Halifax, near the Point Pleasant park, where Mickey would have lots of freedom.

One day, in the cold of winter, they took him for a walk down to the point of the park, where he could look over the water and see Purcell's Cove.

You may have heard of dogs who retrace their tracks to travel to those they love. Well, Mickey, looking across the water at the Cove, must have had some memory triggered in his mind of the Cove and his friends there: the next day he swam the long distance, about two miles, in very frigid water, to come back to me. Of course, we took him back to his folks as soon as he'd been dried, warmed, and cuddled.

Three days later he tried the swim again, but this time he had to dodge between icebergs, albeit fairly small ones, which had been blown into the Northwest Arm from the harbour.

When he arrived at my home this time, we again returned him to his home, but I was very worried that he would not survive another attempt. Mickey, however, was a very intelligent dog, so he did not try that adventure again.

Before long, at the end of the war, it became time for his folks to go home to Montreal, so I no longer had to fear for his welfare. Nonetheless, Mickey's devotion to me will live in my memory forever.

Point Pleasant Park in the background from where Mickey the Dog swam to Purchell's Cove in the middle of winter.

16
Pilot Boats

Pilot boats in The Cove before the road to The Cove was built.

Most of the early photos of Purcell's Cove portray pilot boats anchored there. Obviously they came into the cove for protection from the stormy seas that are so well-known on the Atlantic coast.

These pilot boats were used to transport pilots out to the entrance to Halifax Harbour, so the pilots could board these vessels and safely guide the large ships and steamers into the port of Halifax.

In the early days when a ship was sighted approaching the harbour, the pilot boats would sail out to meet the ship, and the first one to reach the vessel would get the job.

There were many well-known pilots, some of whom were from Ferguson's Cove, Herring Cove, Duncan's Cove, Ketch Harbour, and Sambro. It has been said that one of the pilots had been coxswain on the ship that General Wolfe had sailed on to conquer Louisburg.

It appears the only pilot from Purcell's Cove was William White. Mr. White had the unfortunate job of piloting a famous ship, the Herbert Fuller, with its tragic cargo into port.

It was the summer of 1896. The Herbert Fuller was a windjammer sailing out of Boston Harbour.

There was a disturbed crew member on board who killed the captain, the captain's wife, and the second mate, with an axe, which made a gruesome sight for pilot William White when he

Pilot boat anchored close to William White's residence. It could have been the boat he sailed on to meet the Herbert Foller with its tragic cargo.

boarded the ship to bring her into Halifax Harbour.

The Halifax newsmen were there to meet the ship, but out of a crew of seven they did not know who the murderer was.

Headlines in the paper read, "A Carnival of Murder on the High Seas."

A reporter dug out the information that the murdered captain and his wife had been in Halifax in 1885 and that may have been their honeymoon trip.

The Halifax police questioned the surviving crew and sent them under guard on the steamship Halifax to Boston for the trial. The first mate was found guilty and sentenced to hang.

However, a new law came into effect before the hanging. He was granted a new trial and paroled in 1913, and then pardoned in 1919.

This was not the only tragic incident involving pilot boats.

Herring Cove, lying but a few miles from Purcell's Cove, has seen some significant sea disasters. The people there had watched many an unwary vessel flounder on the treacherous reefs. On March 28, 1940, the pilot boat Hebridean No.2 was sailing out to bring in a ship, for it was the pilot boat's task to guide cargo and troop-ships, freighters and warships, safely in and out of Halifax Harbour.

The Hebridean No.2 was quite an impressive wooden vessel powered by sail and engine.

Just off the mouth of the harbour, a cargo ship, the S.S. Esmond, heading for Halifax, was waiting for a pilot to be put aboard. Her engines were shut down, but momentum was carrying her still slowly forward.

For some unknown reason, the Hebridean moved in front of the drifting S.S. Esmond, which then struck the pilot boat, crushing the smaller vessel which disappeared almost at once.

Boats from the S.S. Esmond, along with a number from the life-saving station at Chebucto Head, searched all night, but only six survivors were found. Since the Hebridean had not responded to wireless messages and had not put into Herring Cove as was the custom, there was speculation it had been in trouble prior to the collision.

One of the victims was engineer bosun Roy Purcell, probably a distant relative from Portuguese Cove, whose wife, that very night, gave birth to a daughter who would never see her father.

Early photos of Purcell's Cove show the Hebridean No.2 pilot boat anchored in Purcell's Cove much prior to this unfortunate incident.

One of the later quarry wharves.

17
Fort York Redoubt

York Redoubt with the Martello Tower upper right.

(PANS)

Purcell's Cove

In the 1790s, Prince Edward, Duke of Kent, the most respected soldier son of George III, landed in Halifax.

He was instrumental in building Fort York Redoubt at Sandwich Point, to defend Halifax Harbour and to protect Halifax from an onslaught by Napoleon.

Edward lost no time in building a version of the round Martello tower on the cliff at York Redoubt.

In this era, wooden ships could be destroyed by cannon balls fired from 24-pounder guns on the shore.

By the 1870s, iron-hulled warships were the order of the day and more powerful guns, firing pointed shells to penetrate the metal plates, were required by the defenders of Halifax Harbour.

York Redoubt was completely remodelled at this time; nine- and ten-inch muzzle-loading cannon with rifled barrels capable of firing 256-pound shells were labouriously raised from the harbour to the gun emplacements on the heights above.

The muzzle-loading cannon being raised from the harbour to the gun emplacement at York Redoubt.
Army Museaum, Citadel

Purcell's Cove

During World War II the fort was manned by the 49th Coast Artillery Battery.

In 1956, York Redoubt was the last fort guarding Halifax Harbour to be dismantled.

Over the years, it had been found that an improved road was badly needed from Purcell's Cove to Herring Cove. This project would link the whole suburban peninsula with a paved road from the Armdale Rotary.

The road, according to the plan first presented, would have to go through York Redoubt, so the fort would have to be demolished.

However, there was a great public outcry about this, and people began campaigning to preserve the fort as a historic tourist attraction.

Following this outcry, the powers-that-be decided to preserve the fort and change the plans so the road could go around the fort.

In 1961, Fort York Redoubt was declared a national historic park. Over the last decade, thousands of tourists have visited and enjoyed the history of this heritage fort.

York Redoubt defending Halifax Harbour (PANS)

18
Early Days and Depression Years

Nets bulging with fish.
(Ruth Iceton)

In the early census of Purcell's Cove most of the men were listed as fishermen, and that was probably the main occupation of most of the residents of the Cove for a great many years.

There were many fish houses surrounding the Cove; the catches were excellent, especially during the herring and mackerel runs, nets being hauled up bulging with these fish in particular.

In fact, Mackerel Cove was the name the local First Nations people had given the place that eventually became known as Purcell's Cove.

Between Spectacle Island and the area known to our generation as Metchler's Point, there is a small channel which was very shallow. In fact, at low tide, I've been told you could almost walk across. In those days, as the story goes, the fishermen dredged this channel to a much deeper depth to permit their craft a much safer entry and exit to the best fishing areas in the harbour. Before the dredging, depending on the tide, a boat might have had to be rowed all the way around the island to gain access to good known fishing spots there.

During the Depression years, known as the Hungry Thirties, when times were bad and in other places people had to go to soup kitchens to get enough to eat, the people of Purcell's Cove had no such problem. There always seemed to be a great supply of fresh fish and lobsters to satis-

Spectacle Island close to the mainland. (Ruth Iceton)

fy our appetites. It may be interesting to note that at that time, lobster, a pricey offering in today's seafood restaurants, was more plentiful and so even the poorest fisherman could offer it to his family.

Also there were many bush rabbits on hand, called by some, snow rabbits because they were not the large jack-rabbits that are common to other places. These bush rabbits made very tasty stews and rabbit pie.

We used to set rabbit snares near our school. One day, having a prospective meal in one of my snares, I was so elated, I went pelting off home with my catch, only to discover later that it was recess, not noon-time break, and I would be late getting back to the classroom.

Moose and deer were more plentiful in those days; they also became staples in our Depression Days diet.

In the woods at the back of the Cove, there were a few game animals. In fact, one time a large moose actually ventured into our neighbourhood; we saw it from our kitchen window. However, it was not hunting season, so moose was not on the menu that day.

The maritime economy had already been

Louie Purcell's wharf with fish shed and lobster traps.   *Longard Collection*

depressed for ten years before the Wall Street stock market crashed on October 29, 1929. I know what the word Depression meant to me; it meant, for one thing, my brothers daily going off to look for work and coming home dejected because there was none to be had. Still, they helped to look after the family.

The winters seemed much colder then, and although we always had a good supply of wood, we needed coal to keep the fires going throughout the night. My brothers knew that when the ships were being loaded with coal, there was always some that landed on the sea-bed. They would go in and dredge for this excess coal.

One day as they were bringing this coal home in the dory, perhaps due to rough seas the dory capsized.

A neighbour, Mr. Will Umlah, had seen my brothers in distress and went to their aid.

He found and rescued my older brother Howard first, and at once Howard said, "Bill's with me too! Where's Bill?" And just then Mr.

Fish nets out to dry. *(PANS)*

Umlah put his hand down into the water and miraculously there was Bill, and he was able to grab him and pull him to safety.

Following this event Mr. Umlah was always invited to come and share Christmas dinner with our family. This reminded us each year how grateful we were to have both our brothers still with us.

In 1918, the oil refinery, now called Imperoyal opened on the shore south of Dartmouth City. The lights from this refinery shone across Halifax Harbour to Purcell's Cove, creating a scene of beautiful harbour lights.

In those years the supply of fish was plentiful and, on the whole, held quite well over the years.

In fact, in 1988, a young Purcell's Cove man, Patrick Purcell, received a government grant to create commercial fishing boats and to help local fishermen in the Solomon Islands, in the South Pacific. Patrick, along with several other Purcell's Cove fishermen, are direct descendants of Samuel Purcell, the founder of the Cove.

Patrick relished the adventure, as he had been involved in third-world projects for CUSO and also for the UN. At present, word from Patrick is that he is very happy living with his family in the Solomon Islands.

In 1887, a petition for a road to Purcell's Cove was signed by property owners of Purcell's and Ferguson's coves, as well as by residents of the west side of the Northwest Arm. This petition stated they were unable to reach the city by land and so needed a road.

Some time later, the House Assembly granted the request.

I do not believe the road was completely finished until the early 1930s.

In 1950, the Purcell's Cove Road received its name formally; prior to this it was called Melville Cove Road.

January 1, 1969, Purcell's Cove along with four other suburbs became annexed to the City of Halifax.

In 1971 a firm, McLaren Atlantic Limited, announced four proposed sites for a pollution control centre for Halifax City and Dartmouth.

The firm had recommended Purcell's Cove as the most likely site for the location of this plant.

My family, along with the residents of the Cove and a very large group of Haligonians, together with the Ward 7 alderman, put up a strong opposition to this plan.

As the story goes, the plan was to push Spectacle Island into the cove to extend the land mass of the mainland. In the process 35 to 40 homes in the area would have been affected. There was great opposition as well, of course, to three other proposed sites, and at the present time this pollution control plant has not found a permanent home.

19
Pier 21:
Doorway Between Our Past And Future

Aquatania sailing into Halifax Harbour.   *(Hilda Lyons Tanner)*

Beginning in 1928, Pier 21 on the Halifax waterfront served as Open Sesame to over a million immigrants, displaced persons, refugees, British evacuees, children, war brides and their children; as the sad departure place for the service people going to the wars; as the Welcome Home to the almost half-million returning troops; and over the years to thousands of Canadian travellers, anxious to return to their native shores.

One of these wartime brides was my own sister-in-law, Sheelah Purcell from the Emerald Isle, who had been living in England when she met my Canadian Army brother.

When this brother, Walter, was coming home at the war's end, he was aboard the troop ship Aquatania, and as they sailed into the harbour his eyes searched for the home cove in the dim light of pre-dawn. The family had gathered there en masse, preparing to drive to Halifax to meet

A barge landing at the Quarry Wharf to pick up stone to build Pier 21.

PANS

Purcell's Cove

The small barge filled with granite stones being hauled up the harbour to Pier 21.　　*PANS*

His Highness The Duke of Connaught at the site of the building of Pier 21.　　*PANS*

The building of Pier 21 with George's Island in the background.　*PANS*

Purcell's Cove

the ship. We made out the shape of the ship making its way into port, so we flashed the headlights on the cars, hoping against hope he might be in a position to see them.

Indeed, as Walter said later, he had exclaimed to his buddies, "There! There's my home and that's my family signalling me."

Pier 21 was closed in 1971 and re-opened in 1999 to much celebration as a National Heritage Site recognizing the last standing immigration shed in Canada.

It should be noted that, although the Pier 21 shed is an important and authentic look into our maritime history, it is the docking pier itself that was built of stone from the quarries of Purcell's Cove.

The construction of Pier 21, including Piers 22 and 23, probably began as early as 1916.

As one of the visitor attractions at Pier21, you will find photographs and passenger lists, and even ship's menus from the past.

As I visited Pier21 recently, the area brought back memories of when my brothers used to take me when they would go to meet Dad when he finished work at the ocean terminals; he was storekeeper and had to be there when the large ships like the Queen Mary and Queen Elizabeth docked.

Such maemories and so many others flood in upon me whenever I cast my mind back to Purcell's Cove and its people and places I loved so dearly. Out of that love this book has grown.

Purcell's Cove as it is today.

George Herb

Purcell's Cove